bewitching
LOVE POTIONS
& CHARMS

bewitching
LOVE POTIONS
& CHARMS

RAVEN TEMPEST

CASSELL ILLUSTRATED

First published in Great Britain in 2003 by Cassell Illustrated,
a division of Octopus Publishing Group Limited
2-4 Heron Quays, London E14 4JP

Distributed in the United States of America by
Sterling Publishing Co., Inc.,
387 Park Avenue South, New York, NY 10016-8810

A CIP catalogue record for this book is available from the British
Library.

Printed in Spain

CONTENTS

INTRODUCTION

Love is one of the most powerful energies in existence. It has the ability to create incredible joy and happiness but in its worst form it can bring about terrible destruction and pain. There are few things that are as everlasting as the magic of love and it is one of the most mysterious and life-changing forces in the world.

Drawing on the best traditions of the East and the West, this book will open channels for inviting, receiving and embracing love and passion in your life. Time and experience have shown that taking the initiative and making simple changes can have the greatest impact and that by incorporating subtle yet effective changes in our surroundings and behaviour we can enable the natural flow of love's energies.

As individuals our strengths and weaknesses vary. While one person is able to express affection and emotion easily, another may find this more difficult. To some, romance is second nature while it comes less naturally to others. By drawing together ancient and modern wisdom, I have provided various solutions and remedies to challenge such problems. Issues covered include overcoming psychological barriers such as lack of confidence and low self-esteem, ways to attract new love into your life, solving relationship problems and enhancing intimacy, communication and passion. Through a fusion of rituals, spells, charms and meditative exercises which can be easily incorporated into every day routines, *Bewitching Love Potions and Charms* will help you find the love of your life and make sure it lasts.

TRANSFORMING A WISH INTO A SPELL

A wish is the seed of a spell and the expression 'you reap what you sow' definitely applies in this case. It is not enough just to hope or fantasize about your personal desires. To turn dreams into reality, you have to transform your wish into a spell but, even then, you need to ensure a successful outcome by the actions you take. For example, if you were to cast a spell to lose weight, it would only work if you took the necessary steps to complement the spell. If you carried on eating too much food, or the wrong type of food, and did not bother to exercise, then the spell would certainly fail. The same principle applies if you were to cast a spell to bring more love into your life. If you simply sit at home anticipating the arrival of that love, the spell would not work.

The idea is that magical spells work in conjunction with the down-to-earth actions that we need to take in order to create opportunities and open the doors to success. Ultimately, it is up to us to take up the challenge and help ourselves.

COMPOSING
THE SPELL

Once you have decided on the spell, the next stage is to compose it. This is a good way of ensuring that your spell reflects your true wishes and that you have covered all the possible loopholes. There are two ways to compose a spell: you can either write it down or say it out loud – or you can do both. Writing a spell has the advantage of giving you the opportunity to change your mind and reword it if you so wish. Always remember to ask for your spell to happen in the right way, and for it not to cause harm to you or anyone else. By incorporating these words into your spell, you are safeguarding the outcome from any adverse reactions, such as the spell working only as a result of misfortune.

A mistake people sometimes make is to worry about the route their spell should take in order for it to be successful. Please leave the small details to the divine powers, they are the best judges. Remember, the sky is the limit, so do not restrict yourself; the pot of gold at the end of the rainbow is well within your grasp.

Creating spells is great fun and, once you have perfected the art, you can begin to create your own. However, before you do so, please make sure that you have read this chapter thoroughly because it is important to know what you are doing, especially when it involves your safety and the safety of others.

DOS AND DON'TS OF MAGIC

DO be careful what you wish for and of the wording of the spell you create and cast. You will get whatever you have asked for, but perhaps not in the way you expected. F`or example, money as compensation for an accident, or even a death.

DO always ask for the spell to happen in an appropriate way and that it shall not cause harm to you or anyone else.

DO cast all spells within a pentacle circle of protection and while you are in the alpha state (pages 12–17).

DO ask for your magic to work for the good of all.

DO take your time with each spell, carefully thinking it through and considering the consequences of your projections.

DO persevere if your magic does not work. It may be that what you asked for may not have been for the good of all. Therefore rethink your spell and try again.

DON'T ever use magic to cause harm or as a weapon to threaten people. Your action and thoughts will come back to you threefold.

DON'T be flippant when you are casting spells. Think carefully about what you are saying and what you project. Use your intuition as well as your intellect.

DON'T cast spells with children or pets in the same room.

DON'T overdo magic. If you cast too many spells in a month you will burn out your magical energy.

DON'T cast spells during an eclipse because the moon will affect the outcome unfavourably.

DON'T doubt your own magical powers as this will weaken your spell.

DON'T discuss your spells once they are released.

THE MAGIC FORMULA
Spell-casting ritual

I will now guide you step by step through the process of shifting levels of consciousness, forming a pentacle circle of protection, and casting and releasing your spell.

1. Shifting consciousness

Sit in front of your altar or in your sacred area and slowly close your eyes, relaxing your mind and body. Once you feel sufficiently relaxed, start by counting down from fourteen to one. As you count, you may experience a tingling sensation. This is the process of your brainwave activity lowering from the beta state(the level our brain is in when we are awake), to the alpha state (when we are dreaming and therefore closer to our subconscious). Alpha is the level at which you are able to tap into your psychic powers and project your spells.

2. Creating a pentacle circle of protection

Once you have reached this level, you need to create a pentacle circle of protection around your sacred area. The purpose of this is to enable you safely to achieve your mental projections without interference from negative, unbalancing, inappropriate energies and forces.

To create your circle, you need to imagine that the divine powers have sent you a ray of silver light. This light is so bright and electrifying that you reach out with both hands and grasp it. The energy of the light will travel down from your fingertips to the palm of your hands and thence to the rest of your body. Next, envisage a bright silver circle forming around you. This circle should include your altar. Then, through your mind's eye (sometimes called the third eye, behind the middle of your forehead), create an imaginary pentacle ⊕ at each of the four geographical directions around your altar.

3. Purifying the pentacle circle of protection

Now that you have created the safety net around your sacred area, you must invite healing energies to purify your circle. This can be achieved by imagining a second beam of light, which is bright blue. This will fill up the inside of your circle, so that it has the effect of enveloping you. It should make you feel extremely relaxed and secure. Imagine all unsuitable energies being washed away.

Spend as long as you like adjusting to your circle. It should make you feel totally calm and confident in your own strength.

Once you feel ready for the task ahead, take a deep breath and slowly release it. Repeat this a few times.

Next, close your eyes, begin to look through your mind's eye and repeat out loud:

> *★I form this pentacle circle of protection*
> *in the name of the divine powers.*
> *I heal and cleanse my circle, so that it is*
> *free of harmful and incorrect forces.*
> *My circle is now ready and filled with*
> *suitable energies for my magical work.*

4. Casting your spell

Then cast your spell as I have shown you. Put all your mental strength and power into the outcome of the spell.

5. Releasing your spell

When you have completed your spell, open your pentacle circle of protection by repeating:

*By opening this circle, I have freed my
spell so that it is successful.
So it shall be.*

Your spell is like an arrow which you have fired into the
universe to land at the right point – and only the sacred powers
know where that is. Once your spell has been released, you
should prepare yourself to return once more to the beta level of

consciousness.

6. Returning to reality

With the palms of your hands open, raise your arms in the air.
Imagine the silver light leaving your body. As it does so, lower
your arms and run your hands over your chakra points (the
power points of the mind and body) beginning at the top of
your head and ending at your feet. Then push your hands away
from yourself. While you are performing this healing act repeat:

*I have now given my mind body and
soul a safe healing clearance. I am
totally healthy and happy.*

Finally start counting up from one to fourteen until you reach beta level. Now that you are 'back on earth', spend a few minutes adjusting.

You have now returned to this world after successfully casting your first spell. Once a spell has been released, it is important to remember never to doubt yourself or the outcome of the spell. To introduce lack of faith in your own ability is to create a rod for your own back and will result in the weakening of your spell.

If you have followed my guidelines, you can be sure that your spells will triumph. The knowledge that you have accumulated, combined with the gift of faith and positivity, should give you a powerful boost. However, such a gift should always be used wisely and with discretion, for every good action is followed by a good reaction.

Before you get ready to go on a night out, light a cherry

incense stick and sit in front of the dressing table. As the

smoke begins to rise, cup your hands over it and collect

the smoke. Release it over your head, face and then the

rest of your body. Envisage yourself in a bright light.

Spend approximately fifteen minutes meditating. This will

increase your confidence.

To bring out your beauty, on a Monday night anoint a

magenta candle with a dab of orange and lemon oil,

rubbing it into the wax. Light the candle and begin to

focus on the colour of the candle and of the flame.

Visualize your beauty being just as rich, acknowledge your

strengths and the positive aspects of yourself.

Sprinkle the following ingredients into a hot bath to enhance attraction – great before a party.

3 drops vanilla essential oil

1 drop ylang-ylang essential oil

2 drops rose essential oil (men may prefer to apply mandarin instead)

Carry a piece of green and pink tourmaline in a silver

handkerchief to overcome shyness.

For courage in love, carry or wear malachite jewellery.

To calm the nerves on a romantic occasion, wear an

amethyst bracelet on your left wrist.

To invite love you need to feel attractive and confident.

Spend time pampering and appreciating yourself. Self-love

is at the root of being loved, so throw caution to the wind

and spoil yourself. As soon as you begin to feel good, you

will notice that it's alluring and contagious.

This spell is to encourage someone who is shy to make the first move.

LOVE KEY SPELL

Essential ingredients

patchouli/strawberry incense

red candle

black candle

key

30 cm (12 in) of red ribbon

MAGIC FORMULA

On the night of the full moon, just before the witching hour, sit in front of your altar.

Light the incense and candles.

While meditating on your wish, hold the key in your left hand and repeat:

The key to my heart is jumping,
So [name the person you want] *take the plunge and get my heart pumping,*

For my heart is oozing love,
And I don't want to be losing your love.
So it shall be.

Then take the key, hang it on the ribbon

and wear it around your neck.

Allow the candles to burn down safely.

Meditation for self-esteem is an important component of

love. Sit comfortably, drop your shoulders and keep your

back straight. Cushions may be used. Light seven pink

candles and some jasmine incense. Using the power of the

mind relax the points of tension in the body and work on

releasing it. Once you have done this spend time

concentrating on the positive aspects of yourself.

The following will help those who find it hard to open up

to their emotions. Create a daily mantra consisting of a

single phrase or a short sentence that is relevant to you.

For example, 'I embrace love'. This may be repeated in

silence or spoken aloud. Repeat the mantra at the same

time every day for as long as necessary.

This spell is for meeting a suitable partner.

CRYSTAL MOON SPELL

Essential ingredients

silver necklace with a pink quartz crystal embedded in it

few drops of lemon oil

MAGIC FORMULA

On the night of the full moon, go outside and stand beneath the moon.

Rub a few drops of lemon oil into the pink quartz crystal and then wear the necklace around your neck.

Cast your pentacle circle of protection, raise both your hands towards the moon and repeat out loud:

I invoke the powerful Moon Goddess to cast this spell.

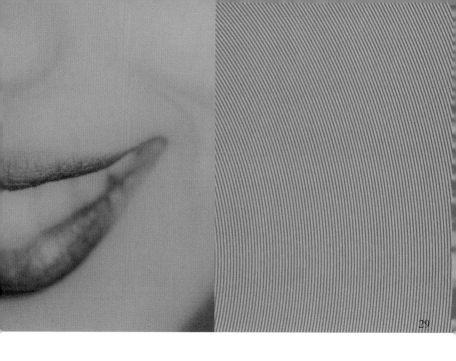

*I wish to meet a suitable partner who will
    enrich my life.
So it shall be.*

Spend as long as you like experiencing the
moon's magic as it empowers you and your spell.
When you have finished, wear the
necklace until you are satisfied that you
have met someone suitable.

If you wish to seduce someone, remember to entice all of

their six senses. Find out their likes and dislikes, impress

and tantalize their eyes and tastebuds using the strength of

colour, texture and taste. Use the power of scents and

music to arouse. It never fails.

This is a powerful love potion which is used for attracting love.

PASSION POTION

Essential ingredients

small saucepan (used only for passion potion)

wooden spoon

chalice or sacred cup of orange-flower/spring water

6 drops rosewater

1 teaspoonful cinnamon powder

1 tablespoonful strawberry leaves

attractive corked bottle

MAGIC FORMULA

Send all adults, children and animals out of the kitchen. Place all the ingredients on or around the cooker/stove.

Once you are ready, cast a silver pentacle circle of protection around yourself and the area where you are working.

Place all the ingredients in the saucepan and, using the wooden spoon, stir your potion clockwise.

Simmer the mixture for approximately seven minutes.

Inhale the powerful aroma of your potion and then energize it by continuously stirring the ingredients.

Then repeat these words:

I motion this potion to bring me an ocean of love
that is suitable for me.
So it shall be.

Once the mixture has cooled, place it in the bottle. Wear a few drops of the potion before you go out.

An auspicious time for meditation for love is on a Friday,

which is ruled by Venus. Near to midnight sit comfortably

with your eyes closed. This exercise is specifically for

removing barriers that may be preventing you from

accepting love and should take you through a journey of

self discovery. Assess the root of the problem then apply

positive visualization and try to see yourself receiving love

and embracing it.

Take a handful of quartz crystals and bury them in the garden and around your home. This will attract good health and love. Meditating on the elements will help improve different aspects of your relationship. Air is often associated with clearing and maintaining the lines of communication. Performing rituals outside using incense are greatly beneficial. Earth is the element called upon to aid in grounding and stabilizing. Fire ignites sexuality and passion, while water is associated with emotions. If you find it hard to forgive, but wish to face the challenge, meditate on the element of water.

This spell will draw loving energies into your life.

STAR-CATCHER
SPELL

Essential ingredients

thin silver bracelet

pink and red threads

brown feathers (shed naturally by birds in fields or parks)

MAGIC FORMULA

On the eve of the new moon, wrap the pink and red threads around the bracelet so that they form a five-pointed star with a single point at the top. The bracelet has now been transformed into a pentacle ⊕

Using either of the coloured threads, attach the feathers to the bottom of the

pentacle so that they are hanging down.
You now have the choice of either
energizing the pentacle with loving
energies or just hanging it in the window
for the Moon Goddess to beam her magic
onto it.

Collecting naturally carved heart-shaped stones and placing

them in the focal point of your living room will draw love.

Meditate using this stone on the positive aspects of life.

Chrysolite is a stone of happiness and luck in love.

While sitting down, light two white candles

and sprinkle cumin around the base.

Hold them both and repeat:

'I deserve love'

then imagine yourself in a better place.

Take a piece of copper jewellery. Rinse it under water

with a dash of salt and leave to dry. Then, while wearing it,

meditate on your hopes and aspirations for love.

Once you have finished this will act as a form of radar

for drawing love.

Adorn your throat with fuchsia, red, orange or silver

jewellery to signal attraction.

This short spell will bring new love into your life.

RIBBON SPELL

*Essential
ingredients*

juniper oil

jasmine oil

30 cm (12 in) each of
green, pink and white
ribbons

MAGIC FORMULA

On the night of the new moon, bathe the
ribbons in the oils.

Energize the ribbons to bring you a new
love that will make you happy.

Place the ribbons together and form one
big knot in the middle of them.

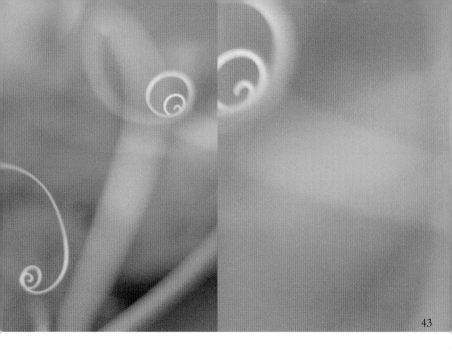

When you have finished and have released
your spell, attach the ribbons to an item
of your clothing.

Build a fire safely either indoors or in the garden. Mix four

tablespoons of myrrh powder, two tablespoons of salt and

one tablespoon of dragon's blood (purchased in any large

herb store) together in a mortar and pestle. While doing so,

visualize the arrival of a new love in your life. Throw the

ingredients into the fire – watch the sparks fly!

This spell is to attract the person whom you desire.

PAPYRUS LOVE SPELL

Essential ingredients

1 tablespoonful raspberry
leaves

1 tablespoonful basil

1 tablespoonful orris root

2 tablespoonsful
rosewater

small bowl

red pen

papyrus paper

square piece of red silk

MAGIC FORMULA

Place the raspberry leaves, basil, orris root and rosewater in the bowl and mix together thoroughly.

Whilst within a silver pentacle circle of protection, write these words on the papyrus paper:

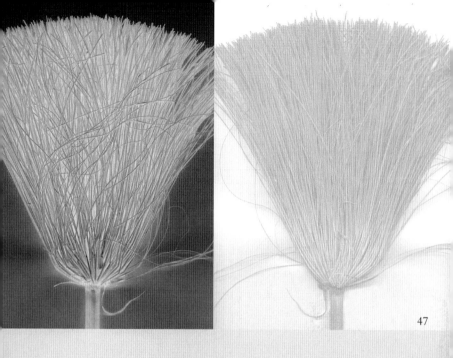

The one I pine for shall desire me as
well, if this is right for both of us.
So it shall be.

Place the paper in the mixture in the bowl, cover
with all the love potion ingredients and imagine
seeing the person you desire.

continued...

PAPYRUS LOVE SPELL (continued)

Say out loud:

O Love Goddess, [name a specific deity if you wish]
bless my spell and sprinkle me with your
love magic and help me to be
the queen of his love.

Then take the papyrus paper out of the
bowl and place it on the red silk.
Tie the corners of the red silk together to
form a knot, then carry it with you until
you feel that the spell is working.
This spell can also be adapted so that it is
suitable for a man wishing to attract the
love of a particular woman.

Write the name of the
person you desire
seventy-seven times on a
piece of unlined paper.
Then burn the ashes and
sprinkle it in the garden.
This will bring them to you.

To attract the love of a specific person, place thirteen red

candles to form a circle. Sit in the middle, light the candles

and envisage your loved one in front of you. After a short

time extinguish the candles carefully and repeat the

exercise every day at the same time for seven days.

Take 16 cm (6 ¹/₂ in) of green ribbon and write the initials

of someone you desire with a symbol of love and a star on

it. Then tie seven knots in the ribbon while repeating their

name. Wear it under your clothes the next time you meet.

This is a wonderful spell for winning the heart of someone you love.

HOLLY LOVE SPELL

Essential ingredients

small branch of holly

23 cm (9 in) red ribbon

few drops of love potion (see Passion Potion, pages 32–3)

MAGIC FORMULA

Energize the branch of holly and the red ribbon to help you win the heart of the person you love.

Imagine your love being reciprocated, resulting in you both being happy.

While putting a few drops of love potion onto your ribbon, say these words:

Love and passion light our way,
Bring me and [name the person you love] *together*
on this day.

But if for some reason it shan't be today,
Bring us together on another day.
So it shall be.

Then wrap the ribbon around the branch and tie it to form
three knots. Leave the branch on your altar until you notice a
favourable change in your relationship. Remember, if the spell
does not produce the desired outcome straightaway, do not
doubt the power of your magic. There is always a reason for
delays and you should not be discouraged; all is not lost. It is
important not to be distracted by small details at the expense of
the main outcome.

Crystals are powerful tools and they have a natural magic

of their own. Take a large piece of rose or blue quartz, hold

it in your left hand and squeeze it. Begin to visualize the

person you seek in love and being happy together. By

releasing your energy into the crystal you are infusing it

with your desire. Carry it with you.

Meditate in a place for love that has a personal association for you. This could be anywhere, an art gallery or even a park. The idea is to focus the energy and channel it into inspiring your love life.

Stand beneath the full moon or a new moon. Observe the power and brilliance of

the moon against the night sky. Make a wish and walk away, ensuring you do not look back.

In the morning make a hot drink and add a pinch of

cinnamon to awaken the senses.

First thing in the morning prepare a hot bath.

Sprinkle three drops of strawberry oil and three drops of

marjoram oil onto the water. Inscribe into a pink candle

the words 'love', 'happiness' and 'passion' and light it. Once

relaxed take in long deep breaths and release slowly.

Repeat this several times.

The colours and textures of
deep red flowers enhance
romance for those in search
of love.

The following flowers are symbols of love, each with a different meaning. Fill your home and garden with them or send them to someone special.

Tulip	*To assert love*
Peony	*To find a long term partner*
Sunflower	*To be triumphant in love*
Lily	*To mend and heal a broken heart*
Plum Blossom	*Luck in love*
Red Rose	*Passion*
Pink Rose	*For self-esteem and self-love*
Orange Rose	*Friendship and love*
White Rose	*To let go of the past*
Hyacinth	*To surround yourself with love*
Bluebells	*Love and magic*
Daisy	*Everlasting love*
Jasmine	*To attract love*
Lavender	*To cleanse a relationship*
Hollyhock	*To succeed in love endeavours*
Daffodils	*To search for new love*
Chrysanthemum	*To bring the fire back into a relationship.*

This is a simple spell to fulfil the heart's wishes.

NINE OF HEARTS LOVE SPELL

Essential ingredients

sheet of gold paper

black pen

nine of hearts (from a normal pack of cards)

box of matches

enamel bowl

MAGIC FORMULA

Cast a pentacle circle of protection, write your wish on the gold paper and wrap it around the nine of hearts.

Burn both items in the enamel bowl,
leaving the ashes until your wish is
fulfilled.

Creating a mandala and placing it in a room where you
spend time is an affirmation of love. You may wish to
dedicate it to someone special or keep it as a reminder that
love comes from within you. You can apply a variation of

colours not only for effect but their significance, too.

Orange *Overall love and strength*
Red *Sex and passion*
Brown *Family, children and home*
Blue *Healing*
Gold *Success.*

This powerful spell will seal the love between you and your lover.

MAGIC LOVE DOLLS' SPELL

MAGIC FORMULA

Essential ingredients

fabric paints

white silk

white candle

basil

cherry oil

strand of your hair

strand of your lover's hair

33 cm (13 in) each of red and pink ribbons

Begin by painting figure, representing you and your lover onto the white silk.

Cut out the figures and create dolls out of them but be sure to leave enough room to stuff them. Within your silver pentacle circle of protection, light the candle and anoint the basil with the cherry oil. Once you have done this, fill up the dolls with basil and sew them up. Using a small amount of glue, attach the strands of your hair and your lover's hair to the

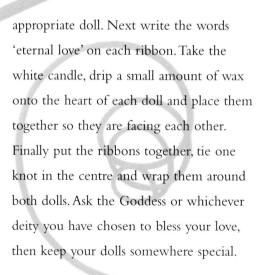

appropriate doll. Next write the words 'eternal love' on each ribbon. Take the white candle, drip a small amount of wax onto the heart of each doll and place them together so they are facing each other. Finally put the ribbons together, tie one knot in the centre and wrap them around both dolls. Ask the Goddess or whichever deity you have chosen to bless your love, then keep your dolls somewhere special.

Inscribe the runic symbol of Berkena into a round fuchsia

candle. Light it and, applying the visualization technique,

direct your mind to growth and development, whether for

yourself or a relationship.

The runic symbol
of Berkena

Take a lump of clay and create your own love runes by

inscribing your lover's name and adding power words such

'love', 'desire' and 'passion'. Paint them the colours that you

wish and place them beside a picture of you both.

Fill a small attractive box full of acorns and sprinkle jasmine flowers over them. This is a significant gift as it will remind your lover of the potential of your future together.

Find out your lover's birthstone and charge it with your

love for them. Then either place it on their desk at work

or in their briefcase. This will give them a sense of

harmony and love and, most importantly, will

remind them of you.

This is a spell for creating a magical present for someone special in your life.

APPLE-STAR
TALISMAN

Essential ingredients

lump of clay

5 apple seeds

red paint

clear varnish

MAGIC FORMULA

When the moon is waxing, mould the clay into the shape of an apple.

Energize the apple seeds with loving, harmonious energies.

Before the clay sets, cut the apple in half and place all the seeds in the shape of a star into one half of the apple.

Mould the two halves of the apple back
together again.

Once the clay has dried, paint and varnish
the apple.

It is now ready to be given to someone
you love as a gift.

a handful of rose petals

1 teaspoonful cinnamon powder

a pinch of meadow sweet

a pinch of lovage

Place these ingredients in a blue pouch and then stash it

inside your or your partner's pillow-case. This will bring

whispers of love to you through dreams.

Carrying moonstone, which is a nurturing female stone, will aid pregnancy.

To increase sexual appeal, dab a drop of English rose oil

behind the ears, on the wrist and the back of the knees.

Watch their heads turn.

Take a garnet stone (women) or a black obsidian (men)

and place it on your base chakra for at least five minutes

every morning for seven days. This will help rejuvenate

your sex drive by stimulating and promoting blood

circulation. Zinc intake will increase the impact.

This spell will add zest to your love life, especially if you have been stuck in a rut.

CINNAMON
SPICE SPELL

Essential ingredients

3 tablespoonsful cinnamon powder

red handkerchief

23 cm (9 in) of red lace

MAGIC FORMULA

Place the cinnamon powder in the handkerchief and tie it together using the red lace.

Whilst within a silver pentacle circle of protection, energize the handkerchief and repeat:

Spicing up my love life, fun in my heart,
Bring me excitement this spell will start.
So it shall be.

Carry the handkerchief in your bag.

I hope you are ready for this spell because

it is very potent.

When you have experienced the magic pleasure of love,

be it the first kiss, making love or a special moment in a

relationship, take a moment to register it in your mind and

heart. At a later stage whether it is a difficult time or you

need to rekindle that love, you are able to reflect and spend

time alone meditating on that special time in your life.

This will help you to take the necessary actions if you

wish to save a relationship. Naturally, if it is an unhealthy

situation and either person is suffering, be it mental or

physical, then this exercise is not advisable.

This spell will increase the love between you and your lover.

MAGIC WOOD SPELL

Essential ingredients

athame

apple

piece of wood (fallen from an oak tree)

pinch of salt

1 tablespoonful vervain

1 tablespoonful yarrow

1 tablespoonful rosemary

MAGIC FORMULA

This spell can be performed either in the home, if you have an open fireplace, or out in the garden.

Begin by building a small fire.

Create a pentacle circle of protection and, using your athame, inscribe your name and your lover's name on the apple. You can also add words such as 'love', 'trust' or 'passion' if you wish.

Repeat the previous procedure with the oakwood.

Now you are ready to place all the ingredients, including the wood and the apple, into the fire.

Spend some time observing the smoke rising from the fire.

Notice the different shapes formed by the flames.

When you are ready, say these words:

Mother Goddess, bless this spell, my lover and I shall be closer day by day.
So it shall be.

Leave the fire to burn down naturally and safely.

For a ritual to let go of an unhealthy relationship, take a

photograph of you and your partner that was taken during

the good times. Go to the beach, stand facing the sea. Tear

the picture in half and throw it into the water. Spend time

listening to the power of the sea and know that you have

the strength to make the correct decision. Walk away.

This spell is for putting the romance back into your relationship.

A SPELL FOR ROMANCE

Essential ingredients

4 peach stones

2 whole nutmegs

wild cherry bark

2 tablespoonsful lemon thyme

6 drops musk rose oil

2 half-coconut shells

MAGIC FORMULA

On the night of the new moon, halve all the ingredients and place them into the coconut shells.

Using your fingertips, mix all the ingredients together in each sell, energize them with romatic energies and repeat:

I awaken the love and romance between
    [say your partner's name] *and me*
So it shall be.

Once you have released the energy, place the
coconut shells in your bedroom, ideally near your
bed.

Creating a talisman out of applewood with the symbol of

the runic figure of Inguz will help achieve a new

beginning. Holding it during meditation increases its

power and helps you to see obstacles as more of a

challenge than a problem.

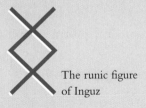

The runic figure
of Inguz

After an argument burn
frankincense and orris root
on charcoal to clear the air
and restore harmony.

This spell will help patch up an argument with your lover.

RED HEART SPELL

Essential ingredients

9 heart-shaped red floating candles

large glass bowl filled with water

MAGIC FORMULA

Begin this spell on a Friday night. Energize all the candles with loving energies and repeat the following while thinking about your lover:

Lover be safe, lover be true,
Lover come back and thrill me through.
Embrace me in your arms and envelop me
in your love.
Let the fire in our hearts bring back our joyous love.
So it shall be.

Spend a few minutes thinking about the
words you have said.

Then place all the candles into the bowl.

Light them and repeat the spell. Imagine
you and your lover patching up the
argument.

Leave the candles to burn down naturall
and safely.

To bring the harmony
back into your relationship
place a thornless rose in the
south-west area of the home.

This spell will help your relationship through rough times.

LIME-LEAF LOVE SPELL

Essential ingredients

2 leaves from a lime tree

pink candle

white candle

black pen

honey

MAGIC FORMULA

On the day of the full moon, pick a few leaves from a lime tree.

Leave them on your altar until the moon is on the wane.

On the Friday after the full moon, sit in front of your altar and create a silver pentacle circle of protection.

Light both candles and, using the black pen, write the name of your lover on one leaf and your name on the other.

Then, underneath both names, write the words 'reunion' and 'happiness'.

Pour a drop of honey on one leaf and place the other leaf on top, so that they are pressed together.

Repeat out loud:

I neutralize the trouble between my lover and I,
    so that we can be reunited and happy together.
So shall it be.

Then place the leaves under your mattress.

This a wonderful exercise for when you are feeling

hemmed in, whether in a relationship or not. On a

windy day sit outside and close your eyes. Feel the wind

against your face and running through your hair. Raise

and drop your shoulders several times. Then, through

your mind's eye, visualize being free and happy. Stay as

long as you wish.

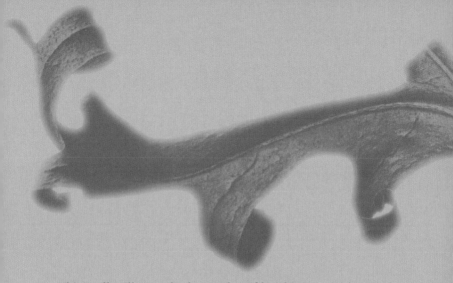

This spell will ease the heartache of breaking up with your lover.

COPING SPELL

Essential ingredients

2 pink candles

3 drops marjoram oil

pink draw-string pouch

7 violet leaves

2 drops cedarwood oil

2 drops tagette oil (obtainable from select herbal shops)

a pinch of sea salt

MAGIC FORMULA

On a Wednesday when the moon is waning, cast a pentacle circle of protection. Anoint the candles with marjoram oil and light them.

Fill the pouch with the violet leaves and add the rest of the ingredients. Using your fingertips, mix the leaves together and rub the oil into them.

Hold the pouch in your left hand and repeat the following several times:

Awesome Brigit, Goddess of the Heart,
    give me your strength to heal my heart.
I energize the pouch to heal my pain, I am now
    happy and balanced again.
So it shall be.

Then, using the sun finger (the third finger) of your right hand, dab a drop of the oil from the pouch onto your heart and over your mind's eye. Close the pouch and leave the candles to burn down naturally and safely. Release the spell and carry the pouch close to you.

To share your life with someone special, it is vital to

balance the male and female energies in the home.

This can be achieved through the design and structure

of the house.

Painting part of the south-west and north-east of the home with bursts of either orange, red or yellow colours will invite loving energies.

Place an image or symbol of the sun, sunset or sunrise in

the southern region of your home. This could take the

form of a painting or any ornament, and will encourage

abundance and happiness.

Placing crystals, particularly quartz, on the windowsill

is effective for drawing the earth's energies, especially

when the sunlight catches it and creates rainbows

around the room.

Keeping ornaments in pairs is a way of ensuring that you share your life with someone special.

Avoid displaying pictures that have images of three people

in them, especially if they include you and your lover, as it

brings about separation.

Get creative and sculpt a statue that represents the meaning

of love for you. Place it in your bedroom and meditate on

it as and when you wish.

Hanging wind chimes in the house or in the garden is excellent for suppressing unhealthy energies.

This spell will help to protect your home.

HOUSE SAFETY SPELL

Essential ingredients

pentacle

lump of turquoise stone

9 bells

MAGIC FORMULA

Cleanse all the items with salt and water, then energize them with protective energies to guard your house from the threats of harm or actual harm, and for this to be done in a good way.

Place the pentacle above the front door of
your house and the turquoise stone above
the back door, and hang the bells from
one of the windows.

Needless to say, you should also take all
practical measures to protect your home.

Take two hyacinth bulbs and plant them in either a

window box or in an earthen pot. While you do this,

concentrate on your specific wish in love. As the flower

blooms, so shall your wish come true. If for any reason it

doesn't work, go back to the drawing board and assess

what you have wished for, then try again.

Placing a statue of Venus or Cupid in the south-west of

the garden will encourage wedding bells.

Avoid keeping cacti in the home, particularly in the

bedroom, as they can cause arguments and create discord.

Place seven red apples
in a golden bowl in the
south-west of the living
room beneath a bright light.
This invites romance.

Keeping fresh coriander (cilantro), basil and rosemary in

the kitchen attracts love. Try using these herbs when

preparing food, especially for a romantic dinner.

It is considered inauspicious to place the cooker and the

sink in the kitchen next to one another, as they represent

fire and water.

Place a mirror opposite the dining table to reflect the food. This has the effect of increasing abundance.

Perform this ritual if you wish to create a magical
dinner for someone special.

DELIGHTFUL
DINNER SPELL

Essential ingredients

mixed-leaf salad and dressing

jasmine flowers

passion flowers

Italian rice

1 teaspoonful red sage

$1/2$ teaspoonful saffron

handful finely chopped
coriander (cilantro) leaves

large tomatoes

avocados

wild mushrooms

several garlic cloves, grated

red wine

olive oil

MAGIC FORMULA

Begin by setting the table and arranging
some gold and red candles.

Energize the ingredients with loving
energies and happiness.

Place the mixed-leaf salad in a large bowl
and decorate with the jasmine and passion
flowers. You may either buy a
pre-prepared salad dressing or create your

own using wine vinegar, olive oil, salt and pepper, walnuts and a dash of French mustard.

Lightly boil the rice until it is soft, rinse it with cold water and drain. Transfer to a bowl and add the red sage, saffron and coriander. Toss in olive oil and leave to one side.

continued...

DELIGHTFUL
DINNER SPELL (continued)

Slice the tops off the tomatoes, scoop out
the seeds and fill them with rice. Then
stand them in a greased ovenproof dish
and replace the tops. Bake in a moderate
preheated oven for 10 to 15 minutes.
To prepare the mushrooms, lightly grease
them with olive oil, add a pinch of coarse
salt and a dash of pepper and sprinkle
with several grated cloves of garlic.

Bake in a moderate oven for 20 minutes
and serve hot on a bed of avocados, either
as a starter or with the main meal.
Pour the wine.
I am sure you can think of a dessert!

Using a compass, locate the south-west corner of your

bedroom and place a handful of natural crystals there.

This will in effect charge the romance corner of

your home.

Avoid having the toilet in the south-west corner of the

home. It has the effect of inviting trouble in love.

Painting the bathroom door a bright colour will

counteract such negativity.

Decorate the bedroom in red if you are in the early stages of love. Apply the colour pink or soft orange, if in a long-term relationship.

Paintings of pomegranates and other fruits such as berries,

cherries and grapes in the bedroom symbolize fertility.

Generally, fruits are luckier than flowers in the bedroom.

Painting symbols and motifs of love on the headboard of your bed is auspicious and will encourage harmony between you.

Avoid hanging mirrors in the bedroom as it may cause relationship problems usually [132] taking the form of infidelity. If a mirror cannot be avoided, then ensure it doesn't reflect the bed.

The position of the bed is also very important in

maintaining a good relationship. Do not place it directly

opposite the door and if possible avoid having the

headboard beneath the window.

Light two strawberry-scented candles and place them on either side of the bed to create a sensual atmosphere.

Take seven cinnamon sticks and tie them together

using a white or a pink ribbon. Then hang it in the

back of your wardrobe.

Plait a lock of your lover's hair with your own and keep it in a special place in your bedroom.

This spell will remind your lover of you.

AMETHYST SPELL

Essential ingredients

piece of amethyst

framed photograph of you
and your lover

MAGIC FORMULA

Go shopping for a piece of amethyst.
It can be any size as long as it catches
your eye.

Take it home and wash it with salt and
water.

While squeezing the amethyst, repeat
these words:

Near or far, I shall be in the good
part of your memory,
Remember me in your heart,

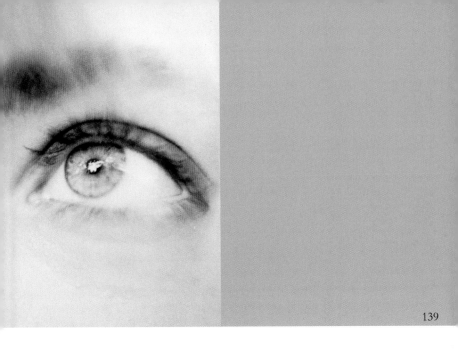

That we shall never part.
So it shall be.

Then place the amethyst in front of the
photograph and draw an imaginary silver
pentacle circle of protection around the
picture and the amethyst.
Remember, always to add that you wish
the spell to happen in a good way.

INDEX

INDEX

ACKNOWLEDGEMENTS

Getty Images: 12, 19, 33, 53, 62, 69, 71, 89, 97, 105
Photonica: 25, 29, 34, 35, 38, 42, 43, 45, 59, 65, 76, 77, 79, 83, 86, 91, 130, 131, 135, 139
Photographers Library: 2, 7, 61, 99, 102, 111
Trevillion: 119
All other images courtesy of Simon Wilder.

Designed by: Simon Wilder
Commissioning Editor: Camilla Stoddart